COMPOSER SHOWCASE
HAL LEONARD
STUDENT PIANO LIBRARY

Florida Fantasy Suite

FOR ONE PIANO, FOUR HANDS

BY SONDRA CLARK

for Marsha Rocklin

CONTENTS

ISBN 978-1-4234-6584-3

HAL•LEONARD®
CORPORATION

7777 W. BLUEMOUND RD. P.O. BOX 13819 MILWAUKEE, WI 53213

In Australia Contact:
Hal Leonard Australia Pty. Ltd.
4 Lentara Court
Cheltenham, Victoria, 3192 Australia
Email: ausadmin@halleonard.com.au

Visit Hal Leonard Online at
www.halleonard.com

In old Key West, the inhabitants keep a quaint and beautiful tradition: each evening the entire village drops whatever its occupations and congregates on the western shore to pay homage to the sunset. Today the practice has been taken up with relish by tourists as well, attracting souvenir hawkers, musicians, and acrobats, creating a circus atmosphere, all joining in the festive spirit.

At last the climactic moment arrives—the sun sets and the people applaud! Then the crowd disperses—some to the cafés to sample the key lime pie, others to the north, where the Latin clubs beckon.

–Sondra Clark

Sarasota Circus

By Sondra Clark

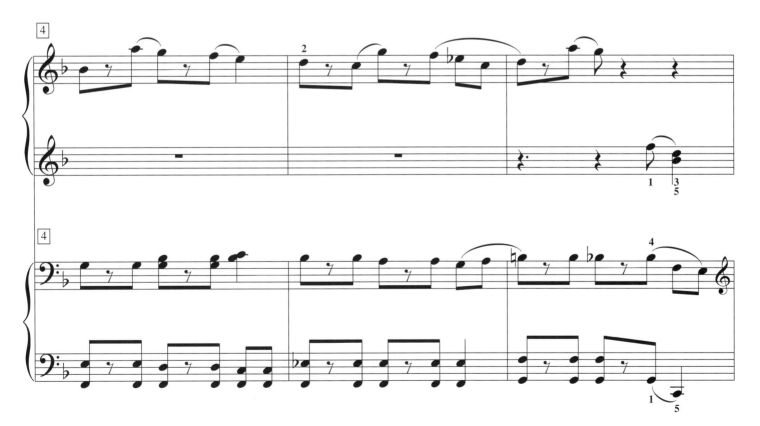

Exuberantly

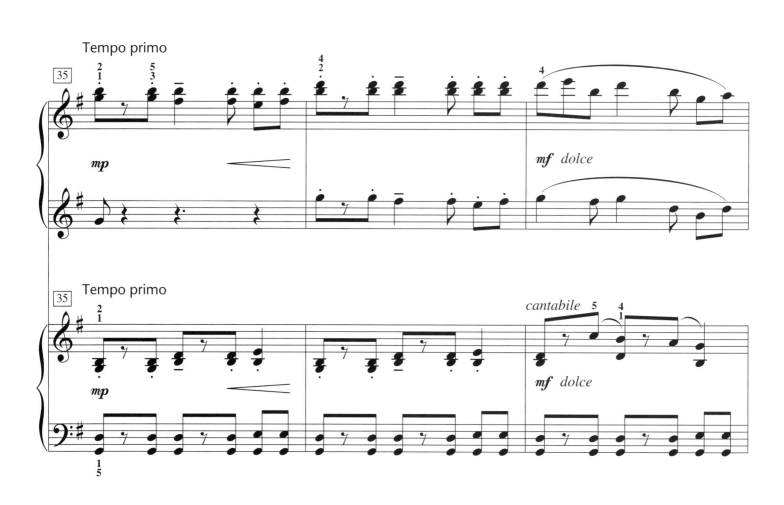

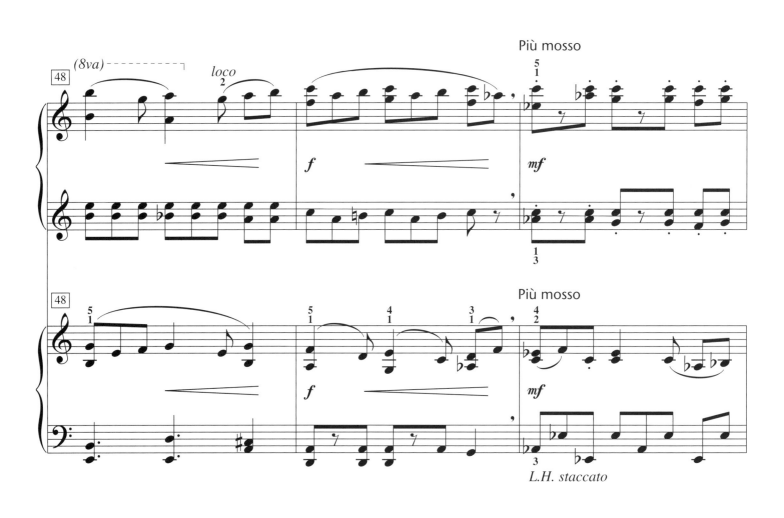

Accel. à la Big Top

Key Lime Sunset

By Sondra Clark

Cheerfully, poco piu mosso (♩. = 56)

Cheerfully, poco piu mosso (♩. = 56)

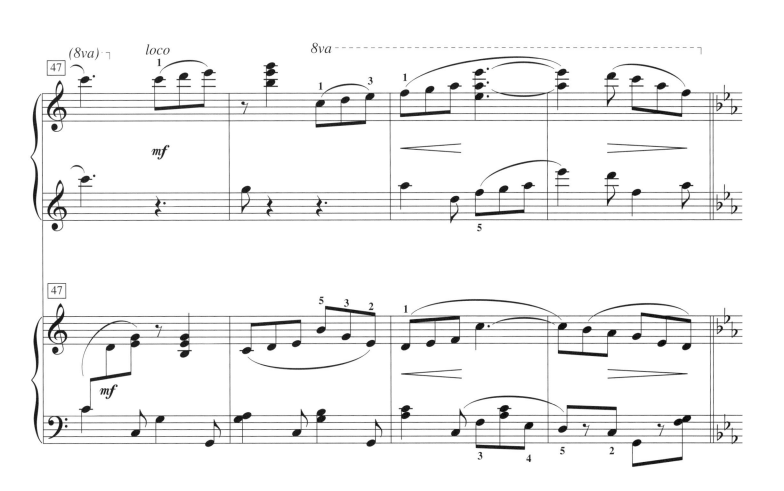

17

Tempo primo (♩. = 52)

Tempo primo (♩. = 52)

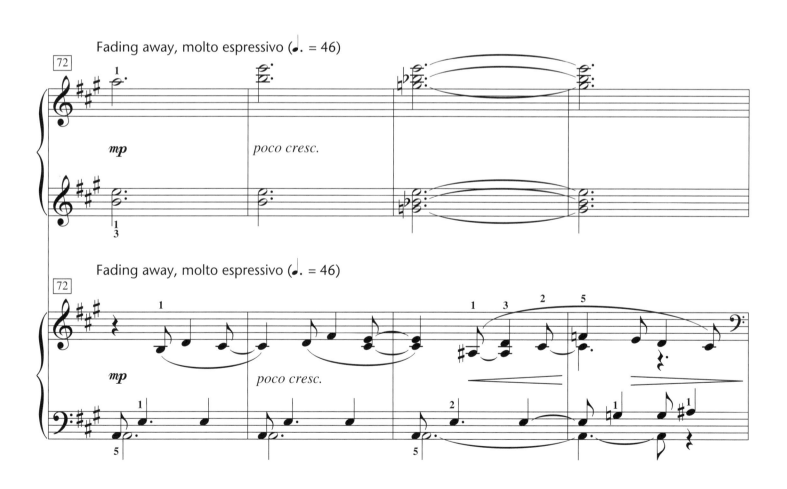

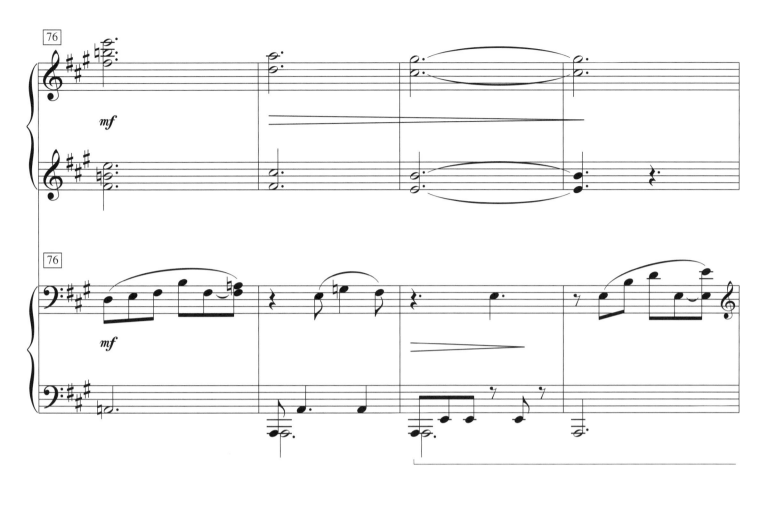

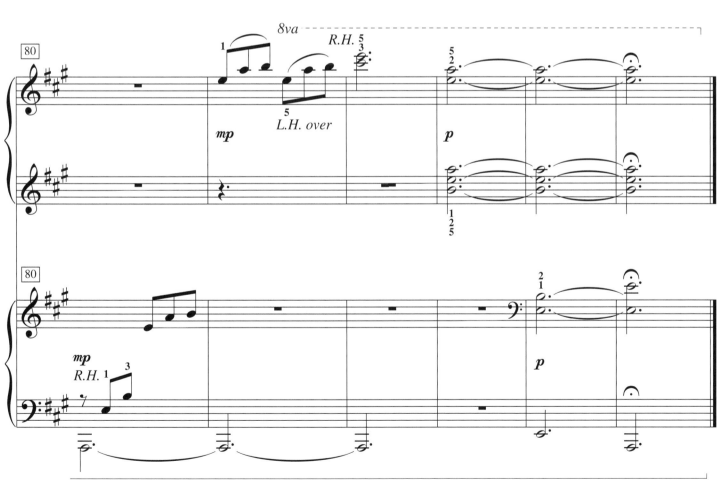

Miami Mambo

By Sondra Clark

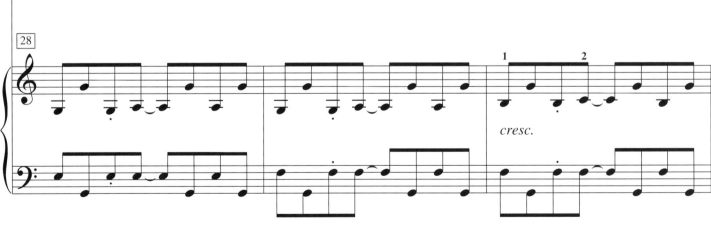

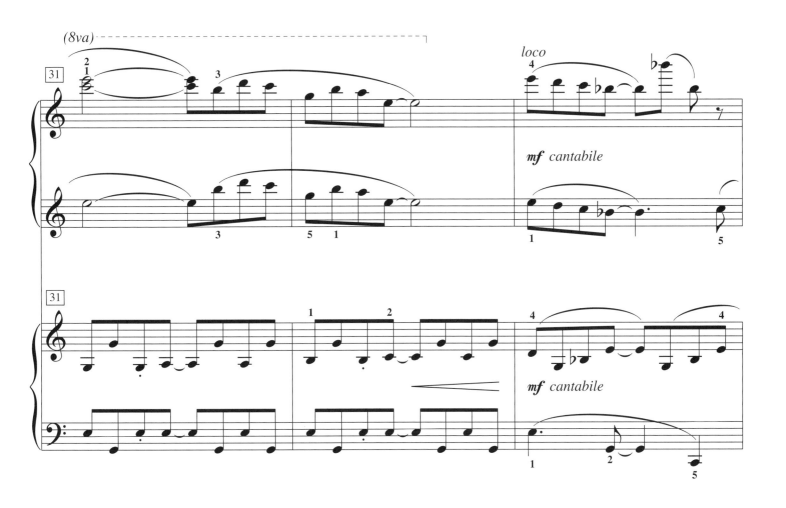

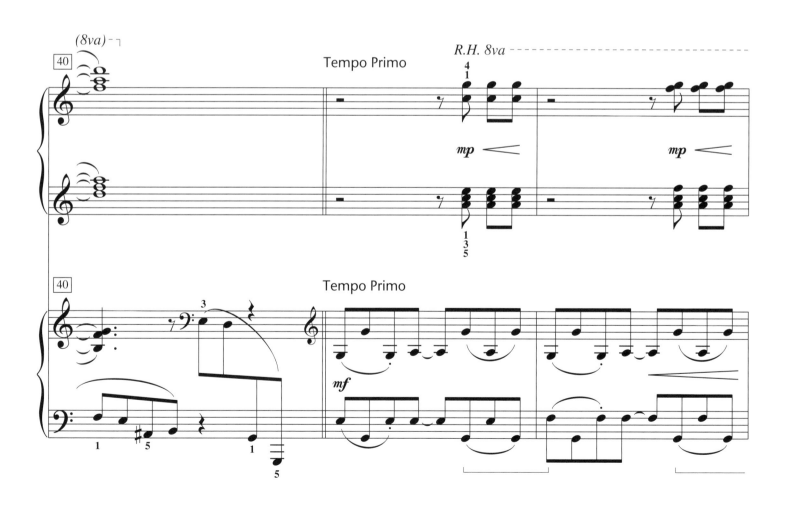

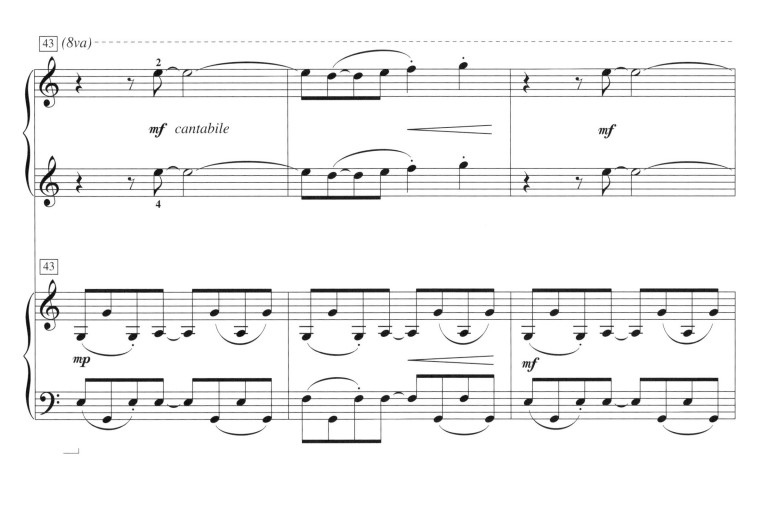

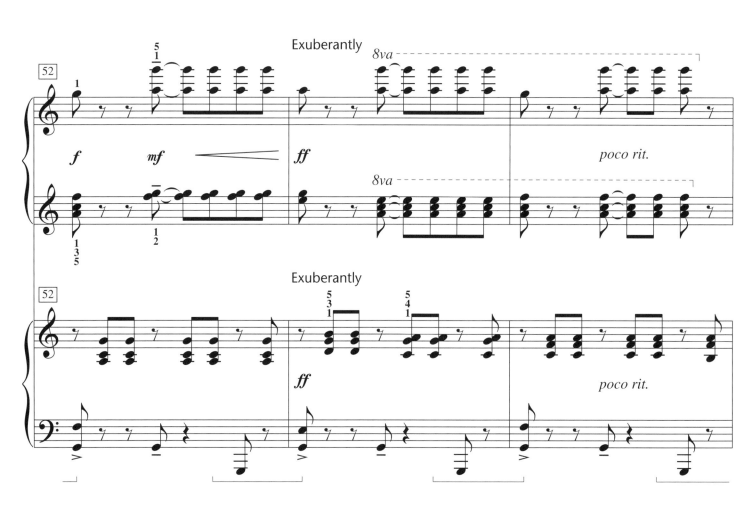

This series showcases the varied talents of our **Hal Leonard Student Piano Library** family of composers.

Here is where you will find great original piano music by your favorite composers, including Phillip Keveren, Carol Klose, Jennifer Linn, Bill Boyd, and many others. Carefully graded for easy selection, each book contains gems that are certain to become tomorrow's classics!

EARLY ELEMENTARY

JAZZ PRELIMS
by Bill Boyd
HL00290032   12 Solos......................$5.95

ELEMENTARY

JAZZ STARTERS I
by Bill Boyd
HL00290425   10 Solos......................$6.95

MUSICAL MOODS
by Phillip Keveren
HL00296714   7 Solos........................$5.95

PUPPY DOG TALES
by Deborah Brady
HL00296718   5 Solos........................$6.95

LATE ELEMENTARY

CIRCUS SUITE
by Mona Rejino
HL00296665   5 Solos........................$5.95

CORAL REEF SUITE
by Carol Klose
HL00296354   7 Solos........................$5.95

IMAGINATIONS IN STYLE
by Bruce Berr
HL00290359   7 Solos........................$5.95

JAZZ STARTERS II
by Bill Boyd
HL00290434   11 Solos......................$6.95

JAZZ STARTERS III
by Bill Boyd
HL00290465   12 Solos......................$6.95

LES PETITES IMAGES
by Jennifer Linn
HL00296664   7 Solos........................$6.95

MOUSE ON A MIRROR
by Phillip Keveren
HL00296361   5 Solos........................$6.95

PLAY THE BLUES!
by Luann Carman (Method Book)
HL00296357   10 Solos......................$7.95

SHIFTY-EYED BLUES
by Phillip Keveren
HL00296374   5 Solos........................$6.95

TEX-MEX REX
by Phillip Keveren
HL00296353   6 Solos........................$5.95

EARLY INTERMEDIATE

DANCES FROM AROUND THE WORLD
by Christos Tsitsaros
HL00296688   7 Solos........................$6.95

EXPEDITIONS IN STYLE
by Bruce Berr
HL00296526   11 Solos......................$6.95

EXPLORATIONS IN STYLE
by Bruce Berr
HL00290360   9 Solos........................$6.95

FANCIFUL WALTZES
by Carol Klose
HL00296473   5 Solos........................$7.95

JAZZ BITS AND PIECES
by Bill Boyd
HL00290312   11 Solos......................$6.95

MONDAY'S CHILD
by Deborah Brady
HL00296373   7 Solos........................$6.95

PORTRAITS IN STYLE
by Mona Rejino
HL00296507   6 Solos........................$6.95

THINK JAZZ!
by Bill Boyd (Method Book)
HL00290417.......................................$9.95

WORLD GEMS
arr. Amy O'Grady (Piano Ens./2 Pianos, 8 Hands)
HL00296505   6 Folk Songs $6.95

INTERMEDIATE

AMERICAN IMPRESSIONS
by Jennifer Linn
HL00296471   6 Solos $7.95

ANIMAL TONE POEMS
by Michele Evans
HL00296439   10 Solos......................$6.95

For full descriptions and song lists for the books listed here, and to view a complete list of titles in this series, please visit our website at **www.halleonard.com**

Prices, contents, & availability subject to change without notice.

FOR MORE INFORMATION, SEE YOUR LOCAL MUSIC DEALER, OR WRITE TO:

HAL•LEONARD® CORPORATION
7777 W. BLUEMOUND RD. P.O. BOX 13819 MILWAUKEE, WI 53213

CONCERTO FOR YOUNG PIANISTS
by Matthew Edwards (2 Pianos, 4 Hands)
HL00296356   Book/CD....................$16.95

CONCERTO NO. 2 IN G MAJOR
by Matthew Edwards (2 Pianos, 4 Hands)
HL00296670   3 Movements............$16.95

DAKOTA DAYS
by Sondra Clark
HL00296521   5 Solos........................$6.95

DESERT SUITE
by Carol Klose
HL00296667   6 Solos........................$6.95

ISLAND DELIGHTS
by Sondra Clark
HL00296666   4 Solos........................$6.95

JAMBALAYA
by Eugénie Rocherolle (2 Pianos, 8 Hands)
HL00296654   Piano Ensemble............$9.95

JAZZ DELIGHTS
by Bill Boyd
HL00240435   11 Solos......................$6.95

JAZZ FEST
by Bill Boyd
HL00240436   10 Solos......................$6.95

JAZZ SKETCHES
by Bill Boyd
HL00220001   8 Solos........................$6.95

LES PETITES IMPRESSIONS
by Jennifer Linn
HL00296355   6 Solos........................$6.95

MONDAY'S CHILD
(A CHILD'S BLESSINGS)
by Deborah Brady
HL00296373   7 Solos........................$6.95

POETIC MOMENTS
by Christos Tsitsaros
HL00296403   8 Solos........................$7.95

ROMP!
by Phillip Keveren
(Digital Ensemble/6 Keyboards, 6 Players)
HL00296549   Book/CD....................$9.95
HL00296548   Book/GM Disk $9.95

SONGS WITHOUT WORDS
by Christos Tsitsaros
HL00296506   9 Solos........................$7.95

THREE ODD METERS
by Sondra Clark (1 Piano, 4 Hands)
HL00296472   3 Duets $6.95

0408